The Sweet Life Series

Wedding Cake Ensembles

Cakes for All Seasons

A portion of the proceeds from the sale of
this book will be donated to
Make A Wish Foundation

World Wide Web - http://www.thesweetlife.com
E-mail - THESWEETLIFE@JUNO.COM

The Sweet Life, Annandale, Virginia

©Copyrighted 1997 by **The Sweet Life.**
ISBN # is **1-891199-00-5**

Edited by Norman R. Davis, Jaci Salisbury, Zane Beg and Julie Morton.
Designed by Zane Beg.
Typesetting by Zane Beg.

Photography by **Grogran's Photo Image.**

Printing and four-color separation by Direct Press Modern Litho
386 Oakwood Road
Huntington Station, NY 11746

Dedication

To Mom and Dad for all the years of putting up with my mess in the kitchen and for all the support that you give me. To Aunt Barb for introducing me to cake decorating. To ~~Jackie~~ Jaci for transcribing all my poor spelling and scribbling and for just putting up with all the things I do at the last minute. And last, but not least, to Zane, for ALL of your help!

Norman

To my husband Don, for his love, patience and encouragement. To my children, Eric, Kevin and Charlene for giving me a reason to learn to make and decorate cakes. To Norm (and his stupendous spit) for asking me to co-author. And to Veronica and Shadonna for being my friends. I love you all.

Jaci

About the Authors

Among their many accomplishments, award-winners Norman & Jaci have appeared in the Washington Post, The Washingtonian, and American Cake Decorating Magazine as well as other publications.

Norman R. Davis is the owner of **The Sweet Life**, a custom-design cakery in Annandale, Virginia. He is a designer of extraordinary one-of-a-kind wedding cakes, a pastry chef, and an award-winning chocolatier, famous for his custom-made molds. You will see a few of his molds in this book. He is a member of the International Cake Exploration Societe & president of Cake And Sugar Artists of NOrthern VirginiA (CASANOVA).

Jaci Salisbury is the owner of **Artistry with Cake**, School of Sugar Art, on Capitol Hill in Washington, D.C. She has been designing, decorating cakes and teaching sugar art for over 30 years and has won many awards. She is best known for her needlework techniques executed in sugar. She has been a member of The International Cake Exploration Societe for several years and is their D.C. representative.

Contents

A Cake For All Seasons

Spring Splendor

Summer Daisies

Autumn Hatboxes

Winter Fantasy

Foreword

Harmony

Weddings are one of the most special events in our lives. Family and friends gather to celebrate the union of two voices singing as one. *Wedding Cake Ensembles* shows you how to bring harmony to the bridal shower cake, wedding cake and groom's cake - for each season of the year.

It's amazing how differently two people interpret the same design. Now that we have achieved our goal we hope you enjoy it as much as we enjoyed creating it.

Introduction

This is not a complete book on cake decorating. We wanted to share some of our dream designs with you. It is our first book, but certainly not our last. This is not a cookbook or a baking book, although we do include a few of our favorite recipes. It's not a book on gum paste flowers, but we hope you will attempt a few. If you're not inclined to work with gum paste, just substitute live or silk flowers. Don't let fondant scare you. If it doesn't work the first time, take it off the cake. Make sure there are no crumbs on it, roll it up in a ball, knead it and try again. If this is your first attempt at making a wedding cake, don't let a project this size intimidate you. Read through the directions well in advance to allow yourself time to purchase supplies. The spring wedding cake is easy for a first timer. Change the flowers and it is well suited for any time of year. Most of the decorations in this book will keep indefinitely and should be made several days in advance. This allows you to work at an easy pace. So, put on your apron, roll up your sleeves, and make an edible work of art that will become a memory to be cherished forever.

and so it begins...

Thanks and Acknowledgments

Abook cannot become reality without the help of a great many people. Words cannot express our gratitude to all the people who encouraged and helped us.

Thank you to Virginia I.C.E.S. for bringing us together. We met at a day of sharing. A very close friendship developed along with a deep sense of admiration and respect for each other. Norman spoke of a long-time dream of writing a book. Jaci had thought about doing one, but never expressed it to anyone. As we got to know each other, we discovered Norman's extraordinary artistic talent for designing and displaying cakes, and Jaci's expertise in making delicate, realistic gum paste flowers and executing delicate needlework designs with sugar. Norman suggested that we combine our talents and do a book together. We both knew it would be a monumental task, but with teamwork and tenacity, we could accomplish it.

Thanks to Ruth & Ed Grogan of **Grogan's Photo Image**, for your expert photography and attention to detail and for capturing the essence of each cake. To Beryl Loveland of **Beryl's Cake Decorating Equipment**, for your help, encouragement and for giving and loaning the essential supplies. To Linda Shonk of **Sweet Art Galleries,** for your donation of all that Choco-Pan™ used for the fondant cakes and for never giving it a second thought. To Tom Bryan of **The Flower Market**, for your beautiful floral designs, and for showing us that simply by changing the type and color of the flowers, we could achieve four seasons with the same cake. To Amir Baig and Linda Schultz for your special support and encouragement. To Addie & Bob Harte of *American Cake Decorating Magazine*, and to Jerry Conrad and Sister Mary Margret (aka Julie Morton) for your hours of proofreading. To Marta Buhay for your cold porcelain recipe and to the Washington State I.C.E.S. newsletter for your Coral Rocks recipe. To Kimberly Lawson of **The Hope Chest**, for the beautiful accessories loaned for the cake photo props. To Jo Soard of **All in Chocolate Shoppe**, for your marvelous chocolate pieces which were used in the photo shoot.

And through it all, there was kind, gentle, hardworking, unflappable and ever-helpful editor and layout artist, Zane Beg. He did the detailed painting of all the animals, arranged the fruit and displays, and kept us laughing through the rough times. He cooked and cleaned for us and was always there when we needed something. He is a rising star on the horizon of cake decorating. Thank you. Thank you. Thank you.

Norman & Jaci

A Cake for All Seasons

The Wedding...

A Cake For All Seasons

No matter what you call it - passion, rapture, ardor, tenderness or affection, it all falls under the name of love. No matter what the season, love lasts all year long. Flowers are given to one's sweetheart as a symbol of everlasting love. Fresh flowers come in a myriad of colors, shapes and sizes all year round. This ensemble goes with them all.

and so it begins...

- Bone gum paste tool
- PME ivy plunger cutter set
- Sugarcraft gun with large cloverleaf disc
- Rolling pin
- 10X (confectioner's) sugar
- Craft knife
- Piping gel
- Pastry brush
- Fresh flowers in season
- 5" cake on 5" cardboard circle
- 8" cake on 8" cardboard circle
- 14" cake on 16" cake drum
- 10 lbs. Blanc Choco-Pan™
- Small, medium and large bow templates (see pattern page.)

Adrian Westrope and Pat Trunkfield teach a class on quilted cakes. This design was derived from their technique.

Roll Choco-Pan™ to 1/4" thickness and cut out full bow and partial bow. Cover bow to keep it from drying out.

Brush back of full bow with piping gel. Place on top of cake, allowing the long end to drape over the edge. Repeat with partial bow, placing on top of full bow.

Add small pieces of fondant where needed to add depth to bow. Smooth all edges with fingers.

Contour shape of bow with bone, flute & vein tools. Cover bow to keep it from drying out.

The Wedding

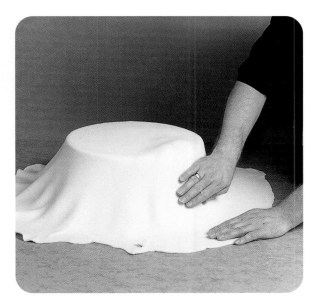

Roll Choco-Pan™ to 1/8" thickness. Brush cake all over with a light coating of piping gel. Roll Choco-Pan™ onto rolling pin. Unroll over the cake to cover.

Pull Choco-Pan™ out from sides of cake to form a tent. Carefully smooth down the sides.

Cut off excess Choco-Pan™ and smooth it over the cake with a fondant smoother.

Cut off excess Choco-Pan™ with wheel cutter.

The Wedding

If an air bubble develops under the Choco-Pan™, stick a straight pin in at a 45° angle. Smooth over the tiny hole and it will disappear.

Mold Choco-Pan™ around bow using tools and fingers. Use firm pressure to give a distinct three-dimensional look.

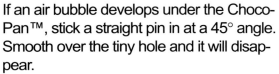

Imprint ivy design (before fondant has a chance to set) on top and sides using the PME plunger/embossing cutter. Be sure to hold the plunger down before pushing into the fondant. We found it easier to take the plunger apart. It goes back together easily.

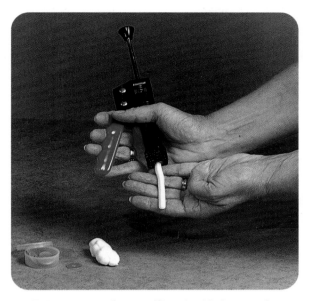

Fill sugarcraft gun (fitted with large clover-leaf disc) with fondant. Push fondant (Choco-Pan™) through gun.

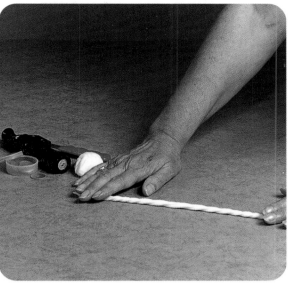

Place on flat surface and twist ends in opposite directions to form rope.

Cut ends at an angle so they will join together neatly and show no seams.

Place around bottom edge of cake with gum glue.

The Wedding

The Bridal Shower Cake...

All tied up in bows, this cake may be adapted to suit the seasons by changing the colors. We chose fuchsia to represent summer's warm, bright sunshine and green ivy to represent its cool evening breezes.

- 10" Cake on 12" cake drum
- 2 lbs. Blanc Choco-Pan™
- Small bow templates (see Patterns)
- PME ivy plunger cutter set
- FMM straight frill cutter set #2
- Spectral fuchsia paste color
- Avocado Lustre Dust
- Rolling pin
- Small round artist's paint brush
- Craft knife
- Wheel cutter
- Piping gel
- Pastry brush

Color Choco-Pan™ fuschia (or color of your choice - *be careful to add color a little at a time.*) Follow instructions for cutting and placing bows on wedding cake, using 5 small bows. Cover cake with Choco-Pan™. Roll leftover fondant to 1/8" thickness. Cut out three strips each with a wide and narrow cutter.

Remove any pieces that did not come out with cutter. A craft knife works nicely.

Cut a straight line with a wheel cutter to form strip.

Gum glue the wide strip on cake drum around the cake. Be sure the strip is touching the cake. Gum glue the narrow strip on top of the wide one.

Emboss ivy around the sides and top of the cake using the same technique shown in the wedding cake instructions.

Paint the ivy using a mixture of lemon extract and avocado lustre dust.

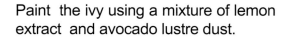

The Groom's Cake...

Rich, dark chocolate to suit a masculine taste. Change the flowers to represent the season. Surround the cake with trails of three-dimensional ivy and you have a groom's cake for all seasons.

- ◆ 10" cake
- ◆ 12" cake drum
- ◆ 2 lbs. Noire (dark) Choco-Pan™
- ◆ Rolling pin
- ◆ Cocoa powder
- ◆ PME ivy plunger cutter set
- ◆ Gum glue
- ◆ Small round artists' brush
- ◆ Pencil or gumpaste tool to shape ivy

Cover Cake with Choco-Pan™ and place on cake drum. Emboss with ivy around top and sides following wedding cake instructions.

Roll Choco-Pan™ to 1/16" thickness and cut & imprint at least 60 ivy leaves. Using the set of PME ivy cutters.

Place leaves over a pencil or tool to form a curved shape. Set aside to dry.

Paint gum glue on the back of leaves and adhere leaves to the cake around the border, top and sides.

Spring Splendor

The Wedding...

Spring Splendor

Spring is the season of birth. New life abounds everywhere with fresh, clear colors of flowers and vegetation. The vivid, jewel-like shades of the tulips and the soft yellow of the daffodils are popping up all over. Spring is also the time when a young man's fancy turns to thoughts of love.

and so it begins...

- 6" cake, on 6" cake circle
- 8" cake, on 8" cake circle
- 16" cake, on 18" covered cake drum
- Rabbit Molds (new product, may be ordered from **The Sweet Life & Beryl's Cake Decorating Equipment**)
- White chocolate summer coating
- 20 cups buttercream icing
- 12" Decorating bag
- Coupler
- Tips #48 & #21

- Spectral paste colors: chestnut, dark brown, mulberry pink & licorice
- Lemon extract to paint rabbits
- Various sizes of round artist's brushes (for painting rabbits)
- Gum paste or silk flowers (You may purchase these or make your own. We made Casablanca lilies, briar roses, yellow day lilies, large orchids, ivy, fern & butterflies. We used Mary Ford's book *Decorative Sugar Flowers* and Jill Maythams' book *Sugar Flowers*, to guide us in making our gum paste flowers.)

This cake is great if you have a time constraints. Both the rabbits and the flowers may be made well in advance. The week of the wedding, all you have to do is bake the cake and pipe a basketweave pattern using buttercream.

The Rabbits

Melt summer coating and fill latex molds 1/4 full. Tip and turn molds to coat entire inside. Place molds in the fridge until set. Do this a few times to build the mold. When mold is full, tap lightly to bring air bubbles to the top. Place mold in fridge until set.

Slowly peel mold from chocolate, being careful not to break any pieces.

If something breaks you can always repair it with melted chocolate. Heat from your fingers will smooth out any seams. Paint will cover any blemishes.

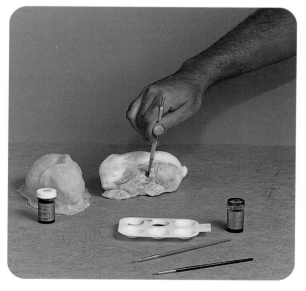

Paint the rabbits. We used Spectral colors (chestnut, dark brown, mulberry pink and liquorice.)

The Wedding

The Bows

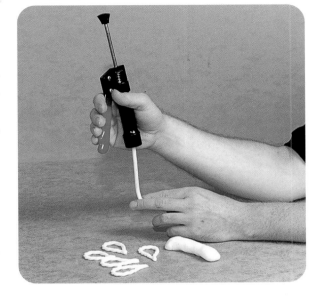

Fill sugarcraft gun (fitted with large cloverleaf disc) with fondant. Make sure the fondant is not too warm or the rope will have a ragged appearance. Press fondant through gun to make a long rope.

Place rope on flat surface and twist. (Roll ends in opposite directions to twist.) Take twisted rope and cut into 3", 4" and 5" pieces.

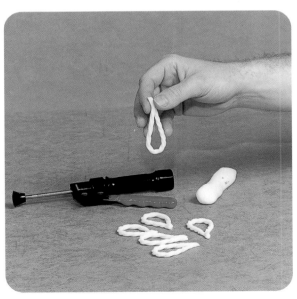

Take pieces and make teardrop loops by pinching ends together. Set aside to dry overnight or longer.

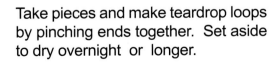

The Wedding

The Cake

Crumb coat all the cakes. Place medium consistency buttercream in decorating bag fitted with tip #48.

Pipe a vertical line the length of the cake. Pipe horizontal lines over this, leaving a space the width of the tip in between. Pipe another vertical line 1/2" from first and pipe horizontal lines over it in the open space from the first set of piping.

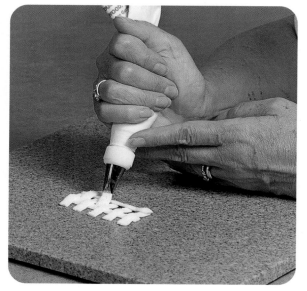

Using any tiered method, stack cakes in an offset manner. Pipe rope borders on top and bottom.

Place rabbits on the base tier.

Arrange the flowers on the cake so that they cascade from one side to the other.

We used gum paste flowers, but you can use either fresh or silk flowers.

Pipe a small mound of buttercream icing where you want to position your bows (you may use fondant.) Position large teardrop loops starting at the bottom of the buttercream.

Gradually use smaller loops as you go to the top. It is easiest to position large loops in the buttercream, let the buttercream dry, and then position the rest of the loops.

Spring Splendor

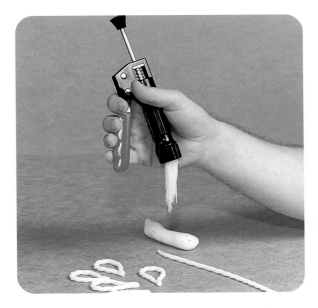

Fill sugarcraft gun (fitted with large cloverleaf disc) with fondant. Make two long twisted ropes. Switch with large mesh disc and push fondant through gun.

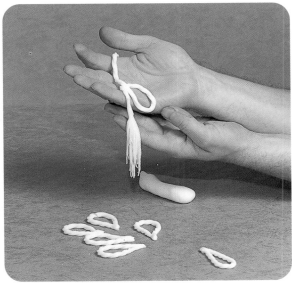

Pinch string from disc. Attach to the end of the rope to create tassle.

Attach rope to area where bow is placed. Position ropes in any bare areas, draping rope halfway down the cake.

Position butterflies on the cake (optional.)

The Bridal Shower Cake...

To contrast the pale, pastel spring colors of the wedding cake, we chose the bright, vivid colors of red tulips and yellow daffodils for the bridal shower cake. The excitement and expectation of the upcoming nuptials are expressed in the flowers that promise new beginnings for the springtime.

- 12" cake
- 14" cake drum
- 8 cups buttercream
- 12" decorating bag
- Coupler
- Tips #48 & #21
- Paste colors: daffodil yellow, tulip red, moss green & purple
- Tinker Tech daffodil cutters #287 & #288
- Gum paste (see recipe page)
- Gum paste tulips (5) & daffodils (7). Use method of your choice. If you don't have the cutters, make cardboard templates and cut with craft knife. (See pattern page)
- Large gum paste bow. (you may use silk flowers and a cloth bow instead)

If you are making your own gum paste flowers, you may make them as far in advance as you like. Make at least 50 purple rope loops (for bows) ahead of time, following instructions for the wedding cake.

Crumb coat 12" cake and place on 14" covered cake drum. Pipe basketweave pattern onto cake following instructions for the wedding cake. Pipe rope borders on the top and bottom of cake.

T h e B r i d a l S h o w e r

Arrange 4 tulips and 7 daffodils in a simple spray and position across the top of the cake.

Pipe a mound of buttercream at the bottom of the flowers where the stems begin.

Arrange remaining tulip and daffodils in simple spray and place at bottom of cake. Pipe a mound of buttercream at the bottom of the flowers where the stems begin.

Place large, dried rope loops around bottom of buttercream bases. Let buttercream dry slightly and place rest of loops (going from large to small from the bottom up.)

Complete the cake with two fondant ropes with tassels. Make the ropes using the same instructions for your loops. Position rope on the cake, curving and loop so that it appears to have just been dropped on the cake.

Fill sugarcraft gun (fitted with large mesh disc) with fondant. Push fondant through the gun. This will make the tassels. Pinch strings of fondant from the disc and place at the end of each rope.

The Bridal Shower

The Groom's Cake...

Delicate is not a word that comes to mind when we think of the groom.   Bold, brave and masculine are much better descriptions. No floral bouquets for him, just rich, dark chocolate topped off with luscious, ripe, hearty fruit carried in a durable, woven basket.

- 10" cake
- 12" cake drum
- 20" wire (cut from hanger)
- Dark chocolate summer coating
- Chocolate Fondant (Regal Ice or Choco-Pan™)
- Regular rolling pin
- 10X (confectioner's) sugar
- Deep Impression basketweave rolling pin
- Gum glue (see recipes)
- Sugarcraft gun with large clover leaf disc
- Wheel cutter (or pizza cutter)
- Small round paint brush (to apply gum glue)
- Fresh fruit – grapes, strawberries etc.
- 2 cups chocolate buttercream to crumb coat cake & help fondant adhere to cake
- Fondant smoother
- Yard stick

Crumb coat the 10" cake with chocolate buttercream and place on the 12" cake drum (we made our cake 6" high.) Do this just before you get ready to put the fondant on the cake. The fondant will not adhere if the icing is dry.

Lightly dust countertop with cocoa powder. Roll out fondant to 1/4" thickness. Roll the basketweave rolling pin over the fondant.

Cut the end of your fondant in a straight line using a wheel cutter and a yard stick. Cut the fondant the same height & circumference of the cake.

Roll fondant strip around the rolling pin.

Gently place fondant around the side of the cake. A fondant smoother will make this process easier. Do not press too hard.

The Groom's Cake

Lightly dust countertop with cocoa powder. Roll out fondant to 1/4" thickness. Roll the basketweave rolling pin over the fondant. Using rolling pin, lift fondant onto top of cake. Smooth and trim fondant.

Fill sugarcraft gun (fitted with large clover leaf disc) with fondant. Push fondant through to make rope for top and bottom borders.

Place rope on flat surface, twist lightly and place at base of cake for border.

Repeat for the top of the cake using thick gum glue to adhere the fondant rope.

The Groom's Cake

Straighten out a wire hanger and snip off a 20" section with wire cutters to form basket handle. Bend wire into a horseshoe shape. Paint wire with melted dark summer coating. You will need to build up several coats of chocolate to cover the wire.

The Groom's Cake

Push handle into cake until secure. When placing the handle, line up the basket weave pattern. Place dark chocolate fondant into sugarcraft gun fitted with large cloverleaf disc and push through. Twist rope and wrap loosely around handle. You might need to use dark chocolate summercoating to keep rope in place.

Arrange the fresh fruit (this is the fun part.) Make sure there are no blemishes or bruises on the fruit. Then polish it. That's right, polish the fruit. Make sure it is dry, then spray a small amount of non-stick coating (e.g., Pam™) onto your hands and carefully rub the fruit. This leaves no flavor on the fruit, but gives it a brilliant lustre.

It is best to arrange the fruit AFTER you deliver the cake.

Summer Daisies

The Wedding...

Summer Daisies

Summer smiles in flowers. Fields abound with dancing daisies. Children make chains with them and many a young girl in love has pulled the petals off while reciting the old rhyme, "He loves me, he loves me not". In the language of flowers the daisy symbolizes purity of thought and for the bride is a symbol of innocence.

and so it begins...

- 1 recipe cold porcelain (see recipes) **Not edible**
- Rose leaf cutter from FMM-029 leaf cutter set
- Glue gun & glue sticks
- 3/4" jewelry pin backings from craft store
- Acrylic craft paint, green & white
- Matte clear acrylic spray
- 14" cake drum
- 16" cake drum
- 2 quarter sheet cake boards
- Fiberfill or gauze Bow templates (see patterns)

- 1/2 ball cake, 6", 9" & 12" cakes iced with white buttercream
- 2 lbs. Wedding White Choco-Pan™)
- Gum glue (see recipes)
- Gum paste rolling pin
- Cornstarch
- Tinker Tech daisy cutter #104
- Tinker Tech cradle cutter #484
- Gold petal dust
- Round artist's brushes
- Decorating bag
- Tips #3 & #6
- Florist foil

Cold Porcelain Daisies

Roll a small ball of porcelain paste to 1/16" thickness on a surface lightly dusted with cornstarch. Cut 60 daisies using cutter #104. Color with gold petal dust and paint small white dot in center and 5 small dots around it using acrylic paint. Let dry overnight.

Color small ball of porcelain paste with a few drops of green acrylic paint. Roll paste to 1/16" thickness. Cut out 60 leaves using rose leaf cutter. Imprint veins using the vein side of the flute & vein tool. Let dry 24 hours. You will need 3 daisies and 3 leaves for each pin.

Glue two daisies side by side on top of a third daisy. Glue bottom tip of leaves under daisies. Spray with matte clear arylic spray and let dry. When dry, glue pin backing to back of daisies.

The Wedding

Bow and Cake Drum

Roll fondant to 1/16" thickness and cut out bow using bow pattern. Bring both ends to the center and gather. Gather underside to meet the two ends. Cut a small fondant strip and wrap around the gathers to form the knot of the bow.

Fill bow section with gauze or fiberfill to open and give shape. Set aside to dry.

Cut quarter sheet cake boards into four 6" x 8" oblong pieces. Stack, placing glue in between each board and cover with glue to bottom of 14" cake drum. This will lift the cake up from the 16" drum to give the base for the cold porcelain daisy pins.

The Cake

Glue 14" cake drum onto 16" cake drum. Place 12" cake on drums. Roll fondant to 1/6" thickness and cut out 288 daisies with cutter #104. Be sure to keep daisies covered with plastic wrap so they won't dry out. Dust daisies with gold petal dust. Imprint diamond pattern all around the cake using cutter #484.

T h e   W e d d i n g

Glue daisies to cake by piping buttercream dots using tip #6 onto the diamond points. Place daisies on top of dots (Do a few at a time so that the dots don't dry out. You will have to cut daisies in half for bottom row.

Pipe 6 small dots of white icing in the center of each daisy. Pipe a ball border on top of cake with tip #6. Place daisies on top of border making sure they are not dried out. Curve them over the top and side of cake. Pipe ball border on the bottom. Repeat with other cakes and stack using any tier-cake method.

Roll fondant to 1/16" thickness. Cut a strip 4" wide and the length of the circumference of the base of the 1/2 ball cake. Gather at both ends.

Wrap fondant strip around the base of the ball cake. The ends of the strip will be the front of the cake. Be sure to choose the best side.

Roll fondant to 1/16" thickness and cut tails of bow approximately 15" long. Gather the top of each one and place on the strip where the ends meet. Drape tails of bow down the sides of the cake and hold them in place with toothpicks until they are dry. Be sure to remove the toothpicks.

Gum glue bow onto top of tails. Fill in open space with a small ball of fondant and shape with the flute end of the flute & vein tool. Place cold porcelain daisy pins on 16" cake drum, leaning them against 14" cake drum all around the base of the cake. Give pins to honored guests as mementos at reception.

The Wedding

The Bridal Shower Cake...

Summer is the season of bright sun and warm days. We chose pink for our daisies to reflect the warmth of the sun and the blush of the bride. We tied it up in a beautiful flowing ribbon and topped it off with a whimsical bride and groom.

- 10" cake iced with buttercream on 12" cake drum
- 2 lbs. Wedding White Choco-Pan™
- Bow templates (see patterns)
- Gum paste rolling pin
- Small round artists paintbrush
- Twinkle pink petal dust
- Spectral past colors: pink, brown & licorice
- Craft knife
- Bride & Groom patchwork cutter
- Gum paste (see recipes)
- Decorating tips #3 & #6
- Buttercream
- Decorating bag
- Fiberfill or gauze
- Gum glue (see recipes)
- Tinker Tech cradle cutter #484
- Blossom cutter set FMM-004
- Tweezers

The Bow, Daisies, Bride & Groom

Make body of bow following directions for the wedding cake.

Make 144 daisies following wedding cake instructions. Dust with twinkle pink petal dust.

Roll gum paste to 1/16" thickness for patchwork cutter bride & groom.

Cut out patchwork cutter bride & groom according to directions enclosed with the patchwork cutter.

Build up bride & groom according to directions enclosed with patchwork cutter. Allow them to dry for 24 hours.

The Cake

Mark diamond pattern on side of cake in a single row around the bottom, using cutter #484. Pipe buttercream dots using tip #6 onto diamond points. Place a daisy on each of the buttercream dots.

Pipe small ball border around top and bottom of cake using tip #6. Place daisies on diamond points around bottom border. Mark diamond pattern on top of cake in a single row with cutter #484. Pipe buttercream dots with tip #6 at diamond points.

Place a daisy on each buttercream dot, curving the daises over the top border. Because the daisies must be flexible they should be made immediately before using.

The Bridal Shower

Add 6 small dots of buttercream in the center of each daisy using tip # 3.

Cut a strip of fondant 4" wide and the length of the circumference of the cake. Gather the strip into thirds. Drape on cake as shown in picture. Hold it in place with toothpicks. Be sure to remove toothpicks when fondant is dry.

Cut tails of bow using pattern template. Gather the top of each tail and place on the top front of cake as shown. Pipe a mound of buttercream in the center.

Place the prepared bow on top of buttercream mound.

Place patchwork cutter bride & groom on top of cake behind bow. Secure in place with buttercream.

Color a small piece of fondant pink. Roll out to 1/16" thickness and cut 20 to 30 small blossoms. Place on cake with tweezers.

The Bridal Shower

The Groom's Cake...

No fragile daisies for the groom! He wants big, bold sunflowers in a vivid shade of yellow. Like the groom, they stand straight and tall, ready to take on any challenge that comes their way.

- ◆ 10" square cake covered with chocolate buttercream on 12" square cake drum
- ◆ Rolling pin
- ◆ Spectral paste colors: buttercup yellow & moss green
- ◆ Sugarflair Sugartex™: nut brown, mimosa & snowdrop
- ◆ Tinkertech sunflower cutters #673 & #669
- ◆ Tinkertech daisy leaf cutters #445 & #530
- ◆ Tinkertech circle cutter #292
- ◆ Gum glue (see recipes)
- ◆ Sugarcraft gun
- ◆ 1 lb. Wedding White Choco-Pan™
- ◆ Crushed vanilla wafers or other light cookie crumbs

Place crushed cookie crumbs aound the base of cake to resemble sand.

Color 1/2 lb. of Choco-Pan™ yellow and 1/4 lb. green. Roll out yellow Choco-Pan™ to 1/16" thickness and cut out 12 sunflowers with cutter # 673 and one with cutter # 669. Keep three of the #673 sun flowers under plastic to keep from drying. Let all others dry. Cut 23 leaves out of the green Choco-Pan™ and dry on a curved surface.

Place soft sunflowers on corners of the cake and mold to the shape of the cake. Place dry sunflowers on the sides of the cake as shown. Place the large sunflower on the top in the middle.

Place some of the leaves under the sunflower petals. Roll left over yellow Choco-Pan™ 1/16" thick and cut out enough of circles for all the sunflowers. Moisten the centers with gum glue and cover each with Sugartex. Set aside.

Place centers on flowers with gum glue.

Fill sugarcraft gun (fitted with medium round disc) with green Choco-Pan™. Push through to make stems for sunflowers.

Place stems on cake for all flowers and add remaining leaves with gum glue.

The Groom's Cake

Autumn Hatboxes

The Wedding...

Autumn

Hatboxes

Autumn is the season when colors are vibrant with rich shades of red and purple or glowing shades of orange and gold. So too, it is a season when colors are subtle - from the palest yellow to the earthiest brown. Alas....it is also the time to put away the beautiful straw hats, profusely covered with summer floral sprays. The perfect places for those hats are delicately-smocked fabric hatboxes.

and so it begins...

- 6", 10" & 12" hexagon-shaped cakes, crumb coated with buttercream and placed on cake drums
- Wedding White Choco-Pan™
- 3 recipes white chocolate modeling dough (see recipes)
- PME ribbed rolling pin for smocking
- 6 1/2", 10 1/2" , & 12 1/2" hexagon-shaped styrofoam, 1" thick, covered tightly with plastic wrap
- Sugarcraft gun
- Craft knife
- Regular rolling pin to roll out fondant
- Gum paste rolling pin
- Straight tweezers
- Gold Lustre dust
- Lemon extract
- Small artist's brushes
- Tinker Tech fan cutter #494
- PME tip #1

- 18" peach color satin craft ribbon, 1/4" wide
- 8" peach color satin craft ribbon, 1/8" wide
- Gum glue (see recipes)
- Gum paste (see recipes)
- Flute & vein tool
- Bone tool
- Tip #3
- FMM-048G embossing set
- Pastry brush
- PME quilting tool
- Small piece of foam
- Small needle-nose pliers with wire cutter
- 10", 14", & 16" cake drums
- Ivy embosser from FMM-048 scroll set #1 Pale, thin, golden yellow royal icing (strained through nylon stocking) for smocking
- Decorating bags
- Paste colors: rust, yellow, orange & moss green
- Foam pad to soften petals
- 3-tier offset or spiral cake stand
- Gum paste or silk chrysanthemums

Gum Paste Gloves

Roll gum paste to 1/16" thickness. Cut out 2 gloves with craft knife (see pattern). Emboss with ivy scroll embosser.

Ruffle wrist end of glove using flute end of flute-and-vein tool. Smooth out edges of glove.

Make 1/4" slits at 1/2" intervals using craft knife.

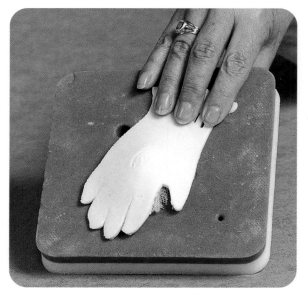

Place small piece of foam under palm of one glove (to shape) and let gloves dry overnight. Weave ribbon into glove (see fan picture.)

Gum Paste Fan

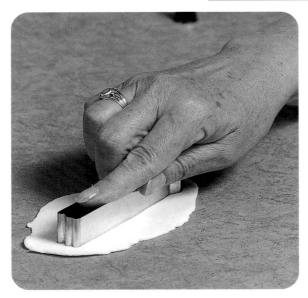

Roll gum paste 1/16". Cut out 18 fan ribs with fan cutter. (This provides a few extra in case of breakage.)

Cut 2 slits, 1/4" apart, in top of each rib using craft knife. Punch out hole in diamond-shaped bottom of each rib using tip end of tip #3. Emboss each rib with ivy scroll embosser. Let dry overnight.

Pull 1/8" ribbon through holes in bottom of each rib, placing one on top of the other. Be very carefull. They are quite fragile at this stage.

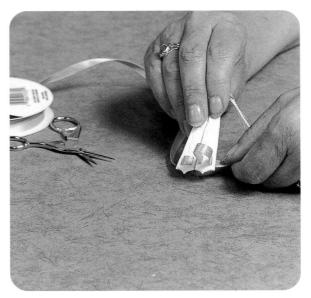

Weave 1/4" ribbon through slits, starting underneath each one and back in over the top. Fan these out as you place the ribbon in the slits to form open fan. Do not place on top of each other. Accent ribs with gold.

We chose to use the step by step photos of the round cake because the degree of difficulty is much higher than the hexagon or square cakes.

Hatbox Lid

Cover styrofoam with plastic wrap.

Roll white chocolate modeling dough to 1/4" thickness. Place on rolling pin and lay over top of styrofoam.

Smooth chocolate modeling dough over the top and mold around sides.

Cut off excess chocolate modeling dough. Place lid on cardboard cake round.

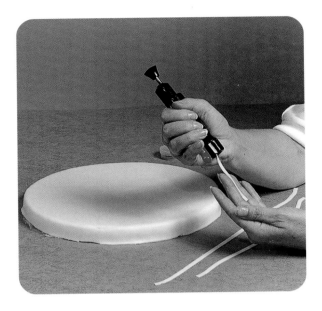

Fill sugarcraft gun, (fitted with medium ribbon disc) with fondant and push through.

Braid fondant using three strips.

Attach to bottom of the lid with gum glue .

Paint braid with gold petal dust and lemon extract mixture. Set aside to dry.

The Wedding

The Cake

Roll fondant (1/4" thickness) into a long strip, approximately 5" wide.

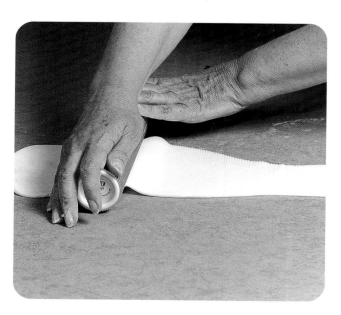

Roll ribbed rolling pin over fondant using a light pressure to ensure that ribbing is prominent. Be sure the rolling pin is well dusted with powdered sugar to keep fondant from sticking to it. If it does stick, just roll the fondant up, knead and start again. Cut the strip the same height and circumference of your cake.

Measure up 1/2" from the bottom left hand side of the panel. To create smocking effect, pinch two ribs together with tweezers. Skip 6 ribs and pinch two more. Continue in the same manner until you have reached the end of the panel. Go back to the left side and measure up 3/4" from the first pinched ribs. Skip two ribs and pinch two. Skip the next 6 ribs and pinch two. Repeat this pattern until you have reached the top right end of the panel. A ruler will help keep your lines even. This is easy but very time consuming and must be done before the fondant sets up. Moisten the back of the panel with water or piping gel and wrap it around the side of the cake. This becomes easier with practice. Be sure to butt the ends up close to each other. This is sometimes easier to do if you make two smaller panels instead of one long one.

Place PME tip #0 in small parchment bag. Place yellow royal icing in bag. Pipe lines like threads from one pinched rib to another in a diamond pattern as illustrated. Pipe two straight lines at each intersection. Braid strips the same way you did for the lid. Place around the bottom for the border.

Fill sugarcraft gun (fitted with largest ribbon disc), and push through. Cut 6 strips the height of the cake.

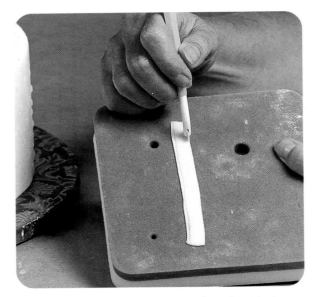

Stitch the outside edges of each strip by rolling the quilting wheel down each side.

Gum glue a strip over each panel join.

The Bridal Shower Cake...

Summer's heat wanes. It is time to pack away childhood memories and begin a new life. Lovingly store your mememtos in a beautifully-smocked box for reminiscing on a rainy day.

- 10" round cake crumb coated with buttercream on 12" covered cake drum
- 2 lbs. Wedding White Choco-Pan™
- 2 recipes white chocolate modeling dough (see recipes)
- PME ribbed rolling pin for smocking
- 10 1/2" round 1" thick styrofoam, tightly covered with plastic wrap (for hatbox lid)
- Regular rolling pin (for rolling out fondant)
- Craft knife
- Straight edged tweezers
- Thin, pale golden yellow royal icing, strained through nylon stocking (for smocking)
- Decorating bags
- PME tip #0
- Paste color : forest green
- Very stiff royal icing, 1/2 cup each: red, golden yellow & orange
- 1 cup thin forest green buttercream
- Sugarcraft gun
- Pastry brush
- Royal icing chrysanthemums

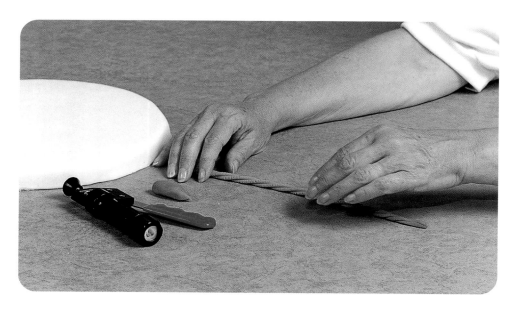

Roll fondant to 1/4" thickness. Follow the directions for the wedding cake to roll, cut and smock the fondant panels.

Color fondant green and push through sugarcraft gun fitted with large cloverleaf disc. Lay fondant on flat surface and gently twist into rope shape. Gum glue rope around bottom of lid and set aside to dry. Place lid on top of cake.

Pipe a mound of buttercream icing on the top of the cake.

Arrange royal icing chrysanthemums on top of the buttercream mound.
Pipe green buttercream leaves in between flowers to finish the cake.

The Bridal Shower

The Groom's Cake....

Carefree bachelor days fade like summer into warm, comfortable contentment. Place boyhood trinkets in this chocolate box and save them for the next generation.

- 10" square cake, crumb coated with chocolate buttercream, on 12" covered cake board
- 2 lbs. Noire (dark) Choco-Pan™
- 2 recipes dark chocolate modeling dough (see recipes)
- Gold petal dust
- Small artist's brush
- PME ribbed rolling pin for smocking
- 10 1/2" round styrofoam, 1" thick, covered tightly with plastic wrap (for hat box lid)
- Regular rolling pin (for rolling out fondant)
- Craft knife
- Straight edge tweezers
- Paste color: forest green
- Thin, golden yellow royal icing strained for smocking
- Decorating bags
- PME tip #0
- Sugarcraft Gun
- Craft knife
- Piping gel
- Pastry brush
- PME quilting tool
- Silicone acorn mold & pine cone mold
- Leaf veiner sets, FMM-045 & FMM- 046
- Leaf cutter sets FMM-049 & FMM-027
- Gum glue
- Cocoa
- Royal icing chrysanthemums

Make fondant acorn, pine cones, leaves, royal icing chrysanthemums and chocolate hatbox lid at least 2 days ahead of time.

Make Chrysanthemums and hatbox lid following directions for wedding cake.

Acorns, Pinecones & Leaves

Mold pinecones, acorn cups and acorn caps by firmly pressing fondant into silicone mold. Press small amount of fondant against fondant in mold. Pull gently to ease fondant from mold. Attach acorn cap to acorn cup with gum glue and set aside to dry.

Roll dark chocolate fondant thinly and cut out leaves with cutters. If you want bigger leaves, use leaf shaped cookie cutters. Place veiner on top of the leaf and imprint veins. Place the leaf in a curved flower former.

The Cake

Follow direction for chocolate hatbox lid on wedding cake, using dark chocolate modeling dough. Roll fondant 1/4" thick. Follow the directions on wedding cake for rolling, cutting and smocking the fondant panels. You only need 4. Place lid on top of cake.

Arrange chrysanthemums on cake and pipe green buttercream leaves in and around them. Paint pine cones, leaves and acorns with mixture of gold petal dust and lemon extract. Arrange on cake with royal icing.

The Groom's Cake

Winter Fantasy

Fantasy

The Wedding...

Winter Fantasy

Winter is the season of short, dark, cold days. It is the perfect time for romantic weddings. Bright touches of flame-colored holly berries nest amongst lush green leaves. Cream-colored poinsettias, and dainty Christmas roses remind us of the joys and beauty of the season.

and so it begins...

- 8" cake on 10" cake drum
- 12" cake on 14" cake drum
- 16" cake on 18" cake drum
- Three-tiered cake stand
- 11 lbs. Wedding White Choco-Pan™
- Sugar Snow (see recipes)
- Polar bear molds (new product, may be odered from **The Sweet Life** & **Beryl's Cake Decorating Equipment**)
- Artist's paint brushes
- Spectral paste food colors: dark brown, chestnut brown, spruce green, christmas red, holly green & blossom tint ice blue.
- Gold petal dust, super pearl dust & lemon extract
- Gum paste (see recipes)
- 1 recipe buttercream icing
- Tip #12
- 28 gauge green floral wire
- Fiberfill (Can be found in craft or fabric stores - used to stuff toy animals.)

- Craft knife
- Flute & vein gum paste tool
- Bone gum paste tool
- Flower formers (Can be made by cutting empty paper towel tube horizontally.)
- Cardboard fruit separator, cut into sections. (Free from the produce section of the grocery store - ask the produce manager.)
- Poinsettia templates (see pattern page)
- PME holly leaf plunger set
- Tinker Tech rose petal cutter #278
- Tinker Tech rose calyx cutter #248
- Rolling pin
- Foam Pad
- Gum glue (see recipes)
- Gum paste holly sprigs & Christmas roses made using your favorite method.

The Poinsettias

Make one each, small, medium & large white poinsettia at least two days ahead of time. They may be made as far in advance as you like; just keep them away from humidity. Make 33 stamens. Let dry overnight.

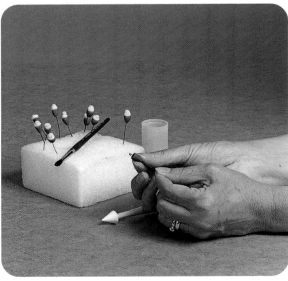

Cut a 2" piece of wire for each stamen and hook the top end. Make a green gum paste cone the size of a small pea. Hollow out the center .

Insert hooked wire brushed with gum glue. Make smaller, white cone and glue into green cone. Glue small ball of white gum paste on top of white cone. Paint ball gold when dry.

Color a golf ball-size piece of gum paste with spruce green coloring. Roll green gum paste to 1/16" thickness. Cut out 5 leaves using template & craft knife. Cover leaves with plastic wrap so they will not dry out.

Soften edge of leaves on a foam pad using a bone tool.

Make veins in leaf with vein end of flute and vein tool.

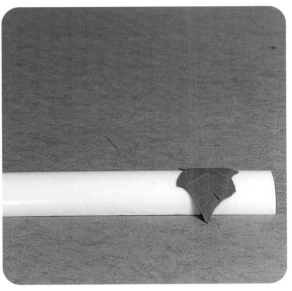

Place over flower former. Repeat process with all five petal templates. Cut five #1 petals, five #2 petals, etc.

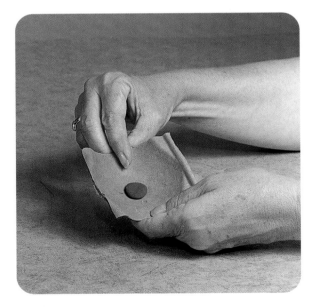

Make a marble-size ball of green gum paste. Flatten it to about 1/8" thickness and place in the middle of the fruit separator.

Place small amount of gum glue on bottom back of leaf. Place on gum paste in fruit separator. Repeat with rest of leaves, slightly overlapping them, going around the flattened ball of gum paste.

T
h
e
Wedding

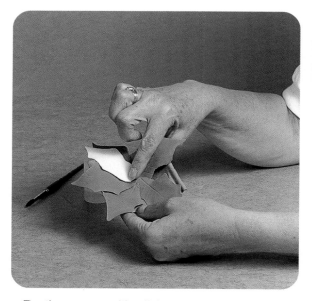

Do the same with all the petals, starting with the five petals #1, then five #2, etc.

Place over flower former. Repeat process with all five petal templates. Cut five #1 petals, five #2 petals etc. Place fiber fill between petals to give petals shape.

Cut wire on stamens to 1/4" length and push stamens into small ball of gum paste. Put 13 stamens in the large poinsettia, 11 in the medium and 9 in the small.

Set aside until completely dry (at least 36 hours.) Pull fiberfill out carefully with tweezers when completely dry.

The Bears

Melt summer coating and fill latex molds 1/4 full. Tip and turn molds to coat entire inside. Place molds in the fridge until set. Do this a few times to build up layers of chocolate in the mold. Fill the entire mold. When it is full, tap lightly to bring air bubbles to top. Place mold in fridge until set.

Slowly peel mold from chocolate, being careful not to break any pieces.

If something breaks you can always repair it with melted chocolate. Heat from your fingers will smooth out any seams. Paint will cover any blemishes. Paint the bears using super pearl dust mixed with lemon extract.

The Wedding

The Cake

Cover cake with Choco-Pan™. Outline shape of trees on side of cake in a zig-zag motion using spruce green gum paste color mixed with lemon extract.

Fill in trees using a dabbing motion. Paint bare trees using a thin paintbrush and dark brown paste color mixed with lemon extract.

Place sugar snow on trees while paint is still wet. Paint only a few trees at a time. You may use gum glue to keep to sugar snow on the trees.

Pipe buttercream in a vertical zig-zag motion with tip #12.

The Wedding

Brush edges out to create snow effect. This can also be done very effectively with your fingers.

Place bears on top of bottom tier. Use blossom tint ice blue mixed with lemon extract to paint water onto tier in front of bears.

Place large pieces of sugar snow on cake to look like glaciers. Repeat with other tiers.

Dampen areas for snow placement with gum glue and sprinkle sugar snow on top ot it. Be careful not to cover the water. Repeat with other tiers. After delivery, place tiers on cake stand and position poinsettias.

The Bridal Shower Cake....

The cake is covered in snow, but the joy of the occasion
is as warm as love. The happily wedded couples journey around the
cake. A bright red poinsettia tops it off for a festive winter look.

♦ 10" cake covered with buttercream
♦ 12" cake drum
♦ 8 cups buttercream
♦ 4 cups finely shredded coconut
♦ 1 lb. Wedding White Choco-Pan™
♦ Large poinsettia template (see pattern)
♦ Mr. & Mrs. Snowman molds (new product,can be ordered from **The Sweet Life** & **Beryl's Cake Decorating Equipment.**)
♦ 12" decorating bag
♦ Spectral paste colors: holly green, licorice, Christmas red
♦ Lustre dust - gold & avocado
♦ Lemon extract
♦ Round artist's brushes
♦ Gum paste holly sprigs
♦ Christmas roses
♦ Tip #12

Mr. & Mrs. Snowman

These can be made a week advance.

Dust molds with powdered sugar. Firmly press Choco-Pan™ into snowman molds. Make sure you get into all the nooks and crannies to pick up all the detail (place molds in fridge to firm.) Gently peel the mold from the Choco-Pan™. You may use white chocolate summer coating instead of Choco-Pan™.

Paint the snowmen and set them aside until needed.

The Bridal Shower

The Cake

Crumb coat 10" cake and place on a 12" covered cake drum. Frost the cake with buttercream and cover it completely with shredded coconut. Position snow couples around the side of cake with buttercream.

Position holly sprigs, poinsettia and Christmas roses on cake.

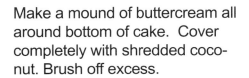

Make a mound of buttercream all around bottom of cake. Cover completely with shredded coconut. Brush off excess.

The Bridal Shower

The Groom's Cake....

One last fling before the wedding.
Penguins frolic jauntily in the snow.
Wow! What a bachelor party!
The ice and snow may be cold, but the fun is sizzling.

- Four 10" layers, filled & stacked,
- 12" cake drum
- Buttercream
- Sugar snow (see recipes)
- Blossom tint ice blue
- Nu silver lustre dust (to paint the penquins)
- Artist's paint brushes
- Penguin molds (new product, may be ordered from **The Sweet Life** & **Beryl's Cake Decorating Equipment**.)
- White chocolate summer coating

Mold four penquins in advance using same technique used for polar bears. Cut one off at the shoulders to place in water. Hold one in hands for a few minutes to soften and then gently bend into an arch to make it look like it's sliding down hill on his back. Paint penquins with mixture of equal parts petal dust and lemon extract.

Carve cake into the shape of a glacier covered with snow. Coat the cake with buttercream and cover with Choco-Pan™. Place on cake drum. Paint water on flat section of cake.

Dampen high areas of glacier (you may use gum glue, piping gel, or water.) Cover with crumpled sugar snow.

The Groom's Cake

Mound buttercream around bottom of cake in zig-zag motion. Using fingers or brush to pull buttercream upward. Cover with sugar snow.

Brush all excess sugar snow from cake.

Pipe small mound of buttercream under penquins and position in place.

Recipes

You may use any of your favorite cake recipes or prepared mixes for the cakes in this book. We do advise that you use a firm cake if you are covering your cake with fondant. I have been using these pound cake recipes for years and my customers always rave about the richness, texture and great taste. Enjoy.

Jaci's Butter Pound Cake

3 sticks butter
2 1/2 cups granulated sugar
5 eggs
3 cups sifted cake flour

1/2 teaspoon baking powder
1 cup whole milk
1 teaspoon vanilla extract

Have all ingredients at room temperature (except milk.) Beat butter until light and fluffy. Add sugar and cream together until a light lemony color. Add eggs one at a time. Beat well after each addition. Sift flour twice. Add baking powder to flour and sift once again. Add flour and milk alternately, mixing well after each addition. Always start and end with the flour. Mix in vanilla. Pour into greased and floured tube pan. Bake at 350° F for one hour or until it tests done with a toothpick. The batter may also be used in any size cake pan. This is a large cake. The recipe may be doubled. Be sure to fill the pans 3/4 full.

Jaci's Chocolate Pound Cake

1 pound butter
3 cups granulated sugar
5 eggs
3 cups sifted cake flour
2 teaspoons black coffee

1/2 teaspoon baking powder
1/2 cup Dutch Process cocoa
1 1/4 cups whole milk
1 teaspoon vanilla extract

Have all ingredients at room temperature (except milk.) Beat butter until light and fluffy. Add sugar and cream together until a light lemony color. Add eggs one at a time. Beat well after each addition. Sift flour twice. Add other dry ingredients to the flour and sift together. Add flour and milk alternately, mixing well after each addition. Always start and end with the flour. Mix in coffee and vanilla. Pour into greased and floured tube pan. Bake at 350° F for one hour or until it tests done with a toothpick. The batter may also be used in any size cake pan. This is a large cake. The recipe may be doubled. Be sure to fill the pans 3/4 full.

Buttercream Icing

1/2 cup solid vegetable shortening	1/2 cup butter
1 teaspoon vanilla extract	2 tablespoons cream
4 cups sifted 10X (confectioner's) sugar	

Cream butter and shortening with an electric mixer. Add remaining ingredients. Mix slowly and gradually, increasing speed to medium. Beat until light and fluffy, scraping bottom and sides of bowl often. For thicker icing, add more 10X sugar. To thin icing to frost cake, add three to four tablespoons of light corn syrup.

Rolled Fondant

When covering cakes with rolled fondant, we find it much easier to purchase ready-made. It tastes good and is easy to work with. However, if you are one of those brave souls with the time and energy, here is a very good recipe for you to try.

1 tablespoon unflavored gelatin	3 tablespoons solid vegetable shortening
1/4 cup cold water	2 pounds sifted 10X (confectioner's) sugar
1/2 cup glucose	2 to 3 drops flavoring (as desired)
5 teaspoons glycerine	

Sprinke gelatin over cold water. Let stand until thick. This is called sponging. Set gelatin mixture in hot water until clear. Heat glucose (one minute in microwave at half power.) Add glycerine and gelatin. Mix well. Add shortening, and sitr until dissolved Place half of sugar in a greased bowl. Make a well in center of sugar and pour in warm mixture. Stir with a wooden spoon until well mixed. Continue stirring, adding sugar until stickiness disappears. Sprinkle sugar on a board or countertop that has been sprayed with vegetable oil spray. Put fondant on board or countertop and knead in sugar and flavoring. Knead until the fondant is smooth and pliable. Coat hands with shortening to prevent sticking. If fondant is too soft, add more sugar. If too stiff add water a drop at a time. Fondant works best if wrapped tightly and allowed to rest several hours. When ready to roll, knead until soft.

Chocolate Modeling Dough

12 ounces good quality semi-sweet chocolate
or good quality white chocolate (finely chopped)
1/3 cup light corn syrup

Combine chocolate with corn syrup, and stir to moisten the chocolate. Melt in microwave at 30 second intervals, stirring each time, for approximately 2 1/2 to 3 minutes. Stir just until mixture is combined. It will look curdled (especially the white chocolate) and broken. This is all right. Pour mixture onto a marble surface or kitchen countertop. Let dark chocolate rest until it begins to harden. It firms up on the outside surface first, so scrape it up and knead it now and then if it hardens. The white chocolate should be kneaded. It will look like it has gone bad. Don' worry, just keep kneading until it comes together. The cocoa butter will pool out. Wipe the cocoa butter up and discard. The dough is ready to use when it is the consistency of firm playdough.

Sugar Snow

Large shoebox   Aluminum foil
4 cups granulated sugar   Water
10X (confectioner's) sugar   1 teaspoon lemon juice
1 egg white or 3 tablespoons meringue powder

Take a large shoebox and cover the entire inside with crumpled foil. Place four cups of granulated sugar in a pan and cover with warm water. Let this stand while you continue on with the recipe. Place one egg white in a bowl. Whip until frothy. Add 10X sugar one tablespoon at a time until stiff. Add one teaspoon of lemon juice. This will be the consistency of royal icing. Put granulated sugar mixture on the stove to dissolve and boil until mixture reaches 260Y F. Take icing mixture and stir into the hot sugar mixture very quickly. Pour the entire mixture into the prepared box. Let sit in the box to harden. DO NOT TOUCH! When mixture is hardened it may be broken apart and used in a snow scene, underwater scene or rock scene. It may be sprayed with an airbrush for effect. If a more solid-looking rock is desired, use meringue powder instead of egg white.

Gum Paste

Several of the flowers, the gloves and the fan in this book, are made with gum paste. Gum paste may be purchased in powdered form in cake supply stores. You just add water and follow the directions. This is easy, but if you use a lot of it, it can become very expensive. Norman uses the ready mix, but I like to make my own. This is the recipe I give my students. I use it all the time. You will need a heavy duty mixer.

Step one   1 tablespoon meringue powder and 1/4 cup water, combine and let stand until it dissolves completely.

Step two   2 tablespoons cold water and 2 1/2 teaspoons (one packet) of Knox™ Gelatin. Sprinkle gelatin over cold water and leave it to sponge.

Step three   3 3/4 cups 10X (confectioner's) sugar, 1/4 cup cornstarch and 1tablespoon gum tragacanth or CMC (gum tragacanth substitute.) Sift together into bowl of mixer. Attach flat beater.

Step four   1 tablespoon shortening (Crisco™) 2 teaspoons liquid glucose. You may use clear Karo™ syrup.

Step five   Gently heat the sponged gelatin until liquid (may be done in the microwave.) DO NOT OVERHEAT.

Step six   Melt shortening and stir in liquid glucose. Add mixture to liquid gelatin.

Step seven   Mix dry ingredients on low speed to combine (NOTE: mixer will be running constantly.) Add the gelatin mixture and 3 tablespoons of Step one mixture (meringue/water.) Continue to mix until all ingredients are incorporated (approximately one minute.) If paste appears very dry, add the remaining meringue/water mixture. Increase mixer speed to medium and mix for approximately four minutes, or until the paste looks stringy, while the beater pulls it from the side of the bowl. Remove from bowl and knead for a few minutes with a bit of shortening. Place in a plastic bag, removing all air, and then into an airtight container. Refrigerate for 24 hours. This is necessary for the gum tragacanth to absorb the liquid and expand to give it the necessary elasticity.

To use:

Bring to room temperature, knead the required amount of paste with a small amount of shortening until pliable. When using, roll out thinly on a hard surface, lightly dusted with cornstarch.

Storage:

Refrigerated, 3 months
Frozen, indefinitely

Gum Glue

This is edible glue used to hold gum paste pieces togther. Mix two parts water to one part gum arabic. Stir and place container into hot water. This should be refrigerated when not in use.

Cold Porcelain

This is used to make non-edible flowers or other objects you want to save. We use this to make the daisy pins on the summer daisy cake.

1 cup Elmer's glue   1 cup cornstarch
3 tablespoons water   2 tablespoons baby oil
2 or 3 drops of white food coloring or acrylic titanium white

Mix cornstarch and glue in a nonstick pan. Add water, oil and coloring. Mix with a wooden spoon and place over low heat on stove. Stir until it forms a uniform mass. Remove from heat. Knead on surface dusted with cornstarch until mixture is even. Shape into a roll. Let cool and then wrap in plastic wrap. Place in airtight container and then let rest one day or overnight. Use the same way you use gum paste. Use Nivea™ Handcreme instead of Crisco™ to make it pliable. Dry objects overnight. Objects may be painted with acrylic paint. For a shiny look when dry, spray with clear acrylic finish. THIS IS NOT EDIBLE.

Royal Icing

5 tablespoons meringue powder or dried egg whites
1/2 cup less two tablespoons water
1/2 teaspoon cream of tartar
1 pound 10X (confectioner's) sugar

Place all ingredients in bowl of heavy duty mixer. Beat slowy until blended. Beat at medium speed until stiff peaks form. Add more 10X sugar if icing is not stiff enough, or a few drops of water if it is too stiff. Be sure to keep bowl covered with damp cloth when not in use (royal icing dries out very quickly.)

Patterns

Bows for "Cake For All Seasons"

Large Bow 1A

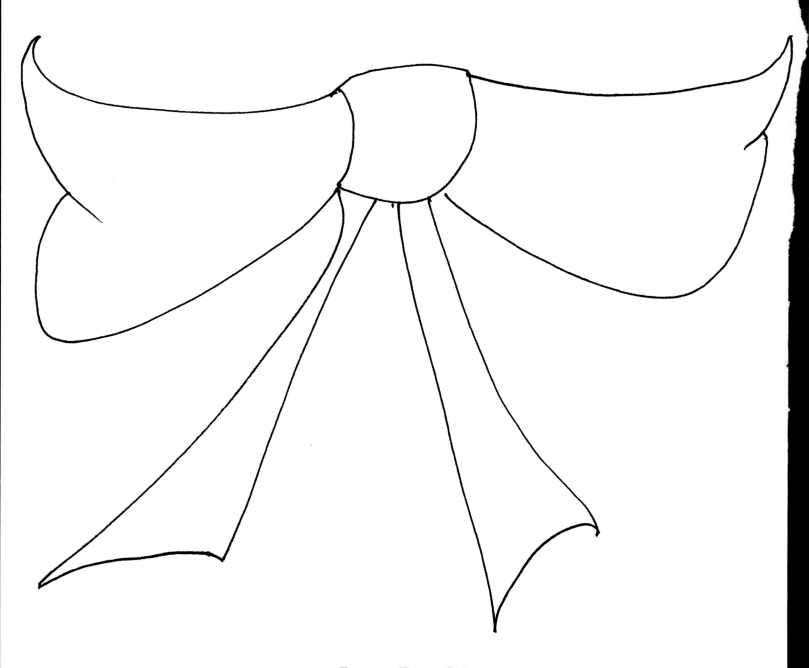

Large Bow 2A

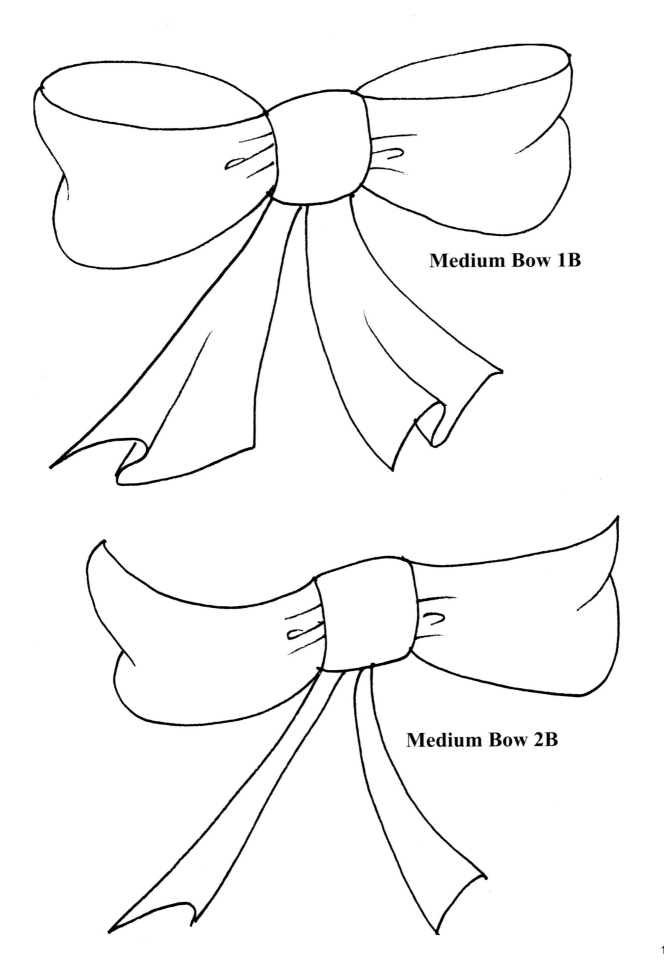

Medium Bow 1B

Medium Bow 2B

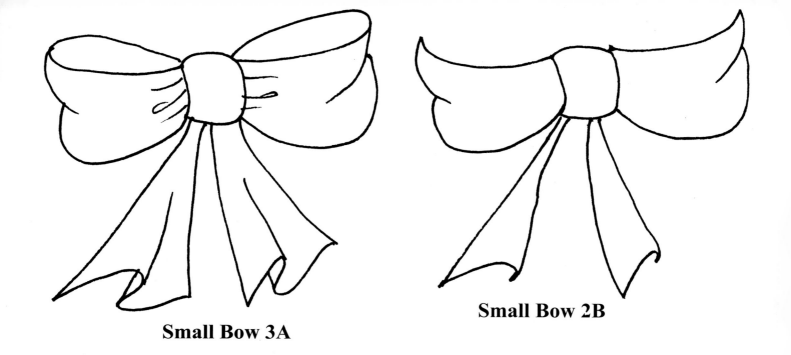

Small Bow 3A

Small Bow 2B

Poinsettias For "Winter Cake"

Leaf

Petal #1

Petal #2

Petal #3

Petal #4

Petal #5

Medium Flower

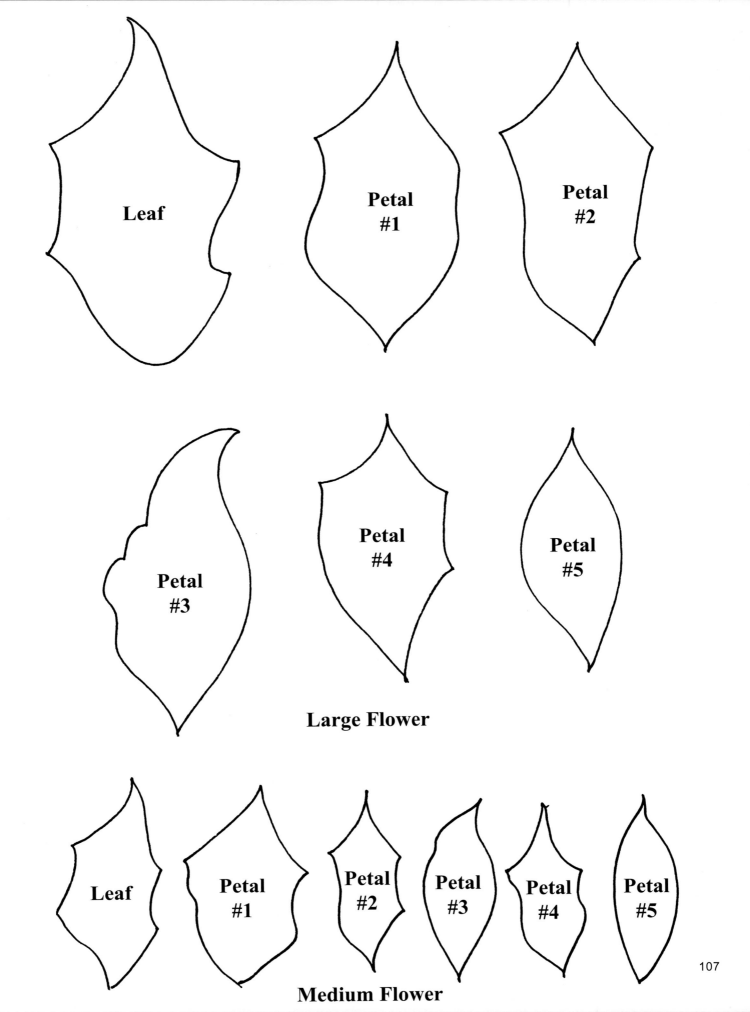

Leaf

Petal #1

Petal #2

Petal #3

Petal #4

Petal #5

Large Flower

Leaf

Petal #1

Petal #2

Petal #3

Petal #4

Petal #5

Medium Flower

107

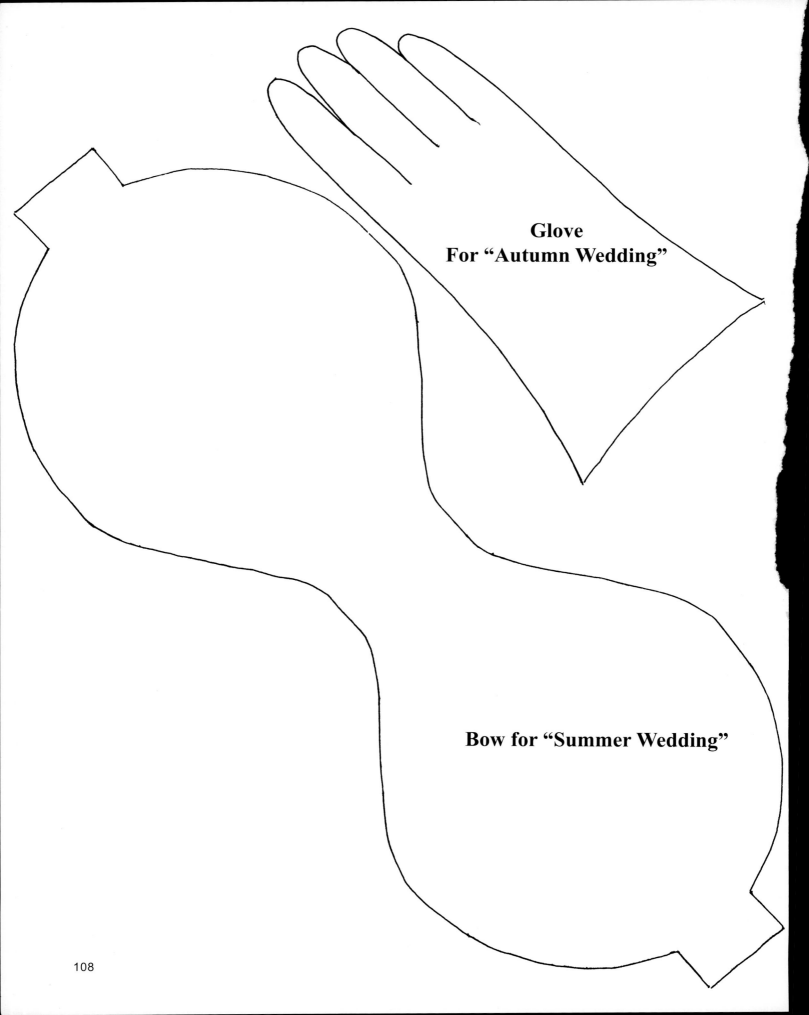

**Glove
For "Autumn Wedding"**

Bow for "Summer Wedding"

108

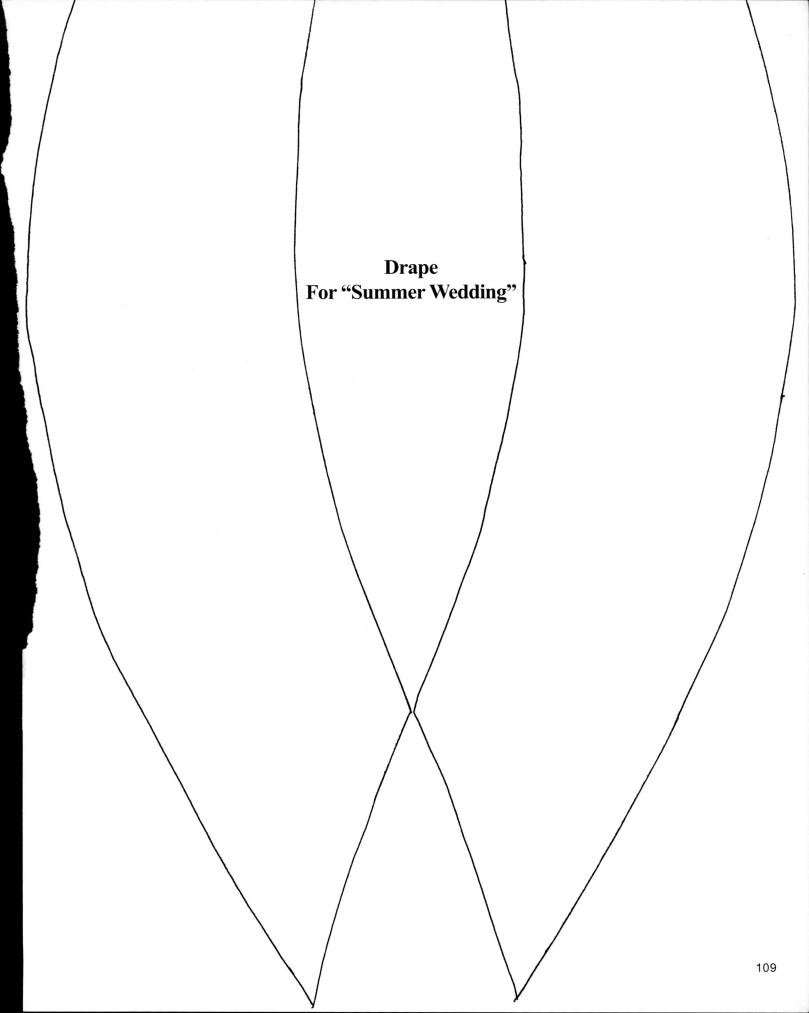

Drape
For "Summer Wedding"

Supply Sources

Speciality Chocolates (custom-made chocolate logos, chocolate brochures and candies) in any shape, size, and quantity. Will ship anywhere.
All In Chocolate Shoppe
1521 King Street
Alexandria, VA 22314
Tel: (703) 739-7777

For subscriptions to:
American Cake Decorating
P.O. Box 21645
Eagan, MN 52121-0645
Tel: (703) 430-2356
Internet: http://www.cakemag.com

Brochures for Sugar Art classes:
Artistry With Cake
647 F Street, N.E.
Washington, D.C. 20002-5217
Tel: (202) 544-1917
E-mail: cake.designer@mindspring.com

Confection Connection for Imported British Decorating Supplies:
Beryl's Cake Decorating Equipment
P. O. Box 1584
North Springfield, VA 22151
Tel: (703) 256-6951 and
1-800-488-2749
Fax: (703) 750-3779
E-mail: beryls@beryls.com

English Country Floral Designs:
The Flower Market
322 South Washington Street
Old Town Alexandria, VA 22314
Tel: (703) 684-2144 and
1-800-776-9585
Fax: (703) 684-3924

Fine Photography:
Grogins Photo Image
2837 Summerfield Road
Falls Church, VA 22042
(703) 534-2861
Fax: (703) 536-2528

Bridal Accessories:
The Hope Chest
628 N. Washington Street
Old Town Alexandria, VA 22314
Tel: (703) 681-0111

International Cake Exploration Societey
I.C.E.S. Membership:
1740 44th Street S.W.
Wyoming, MI 49504
Internet: http://www.ices.org.

Choco-Pan™
(chocolate rolled fondant):
Sweet Art Galleries
Suite A, 5575 Elmwood Drive
Indianapolis, IN 46203
Tel: (317) 787-3647
Fax: (317) 787-3702

Custom-made molds and personally autographed copies of *Wedding Cake Ensembles*
The Sweet Life
6703 Perry Penny Drive
Annandale, VA 22003
Tel: (703) 750-3266
Fax: (703) 642-8878
Internet: http://www.thesweetlife.com

Glossary

BLOSSOM CUTTER - Used to make small flowers which are useful as an individual decoration as well as for combining with larger blossoms. Cutters are made of metal or plastic and they are used to stamp out flowers in one piece. Some blossom cutters are the plunger type, incorporating a spring-loaded plunger with the cutter to curve the flower for realism.

CAKE DRUM - British cake boards. Much more sturdier than cardboard separators. May be used as the separator plate between cake tiers instead of the usual plastic plate or as the board on which to decorate and serve your cake.

CHOCOLATE or SUMMER COATING - Contains cocoa butter, sugar milk solids and flavorings. Does not contain any non-fat cocoa solids. Does not need to be tempered and melts at a higher temperature than chocolate.

EMBOSSER - Small implement with a relief design on its surface, used to stamp a pattern into fondant, gum paste or pastillage. The design may be colored by painting with food color or petal dust. (Quick tip: buttons, badges and other firm items which have a raised pattern are suitable for making impressions into fondant.)

FONDANT - The original name dating back to the 1600's is Sugar Paste. This is a soft, pliable paste which is rolled out and used to form a smooth coating on a cake or plaque. Generally, white fondant is easily colored. There is considerable confusion over the various names which are used for fondant. It is particularly versatile and it can be used for covering cakes, making plaques, modeling flowers and animals and for making frills. It can also be flavored to make cut out sweets or centers for chocolates.

GELATINE - A substance extacted from protein in bones. Available in two forms, powdered, which is most common, and leaf. Always add gelatin to the liquid, not the other way around. Sprinkle over cold water (do not stir), and let mixture stand for 15 minutes. By then the gelatin will have absorbed the water and swollen to a spongy consistency. This process is known as sponging.

GUM ARABIC - A pale-colored powder obtained from the acacia tree. Gum arabic is available from specialty cake decorating supply stores. It is most often used to make gum glue.

GUMPASTE - Also referred to as Flower Paste. Used primarily for hand-modeled flowers. It is also used for other decorations. There are many recipes for making the paste, which should include gum tragacanth or CMC (gum tragacanth substitute). This gum strengthens the paste and enables it to be rolled out until it is transclucent.

GUM TRAGACANTH - A gum extracted from a small tree or bush found in Mediterranean countries, including Greece, Turkey and Syria. The name is derived from tragakantha. Tra-os (goat) and akantha (thorn). It is available as a cream-colored powder which expands when moistened. It is expensive but only a small amount is needed to stiffen paste.

LIQUID GLUCOSE - Also known as corn syrup or clear corn syrup. Liquid glucose has a thick, syrupy texture and it becomes runny when warmed.

MODELING TOOLS - Invaluable help for modeling flowers. They may be purchased singly or in sets.
Bone tool - Each end has a different size ball for marking eye sockets, curving petals, making open mouths or thinning petals ofsmall flowers.
Flute & Vein Tool - Flute side used to frill edge of small flower petals and veiner for making veins in leaves and some flowers.

PETAL DUST - Also known as blossom tint and dusting powder. Fine powders in pale and deep colors. Used for dusting on flowers or a dry, iced surface to give a background tint or variation in shades of color. They are also useful for dusting the edge of frills. Different powders may be mixed to create a wide variety of colors. Dark colors may be lightened by the addition of cornstarch. Silver and gold luster add a glamorous sparkle to celebration cakes.

SUGARPASTE - See fondant.